*commissioned by the Choir Schools' Association
celebrating the year 2000*

Love divir

Text by Charles Wesley

(Repeat ppp)   pp

16

All thy faith - ful mer - cies crown.
Let us find that se - cond rest:

19

mf

Je - su, thou art all com - pas - sion, Pure un - bound - ed
Take a - way our power of sin - ning, Al - pha and O -

mf

Je - su, thou art all com - pas - sion, Pure un - bound - ed
Take a - way our power of sin - ning, Al - pha and O -

mf

Je - su, thou art all com - pas - sion, Pure un - bound - ed
Take a - way our power of sin - ning, Al - pha and O -

mf

Je - su, thou art all com - pas - sion, Pure un - bound - ed
Take a - way our power of sin - ning, Al - pha and O -

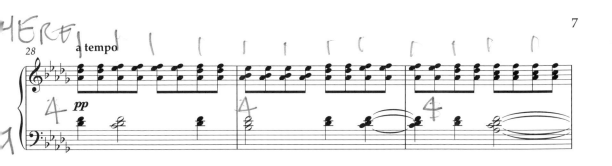

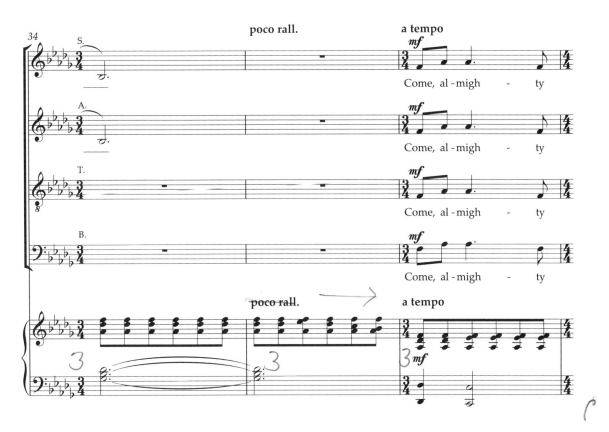

tem - ples leave. Thee we would be

tem - ples leave. Thee we would be

tem - ples leave. Thee we would be

tem - ples leave. Thee we would be

al - ways bless - ing, Serve thee as thy hosts a - bove;

al - ways bless - ing, Serve thee as thy hosts a - bove;

al - ways bless - ing, Serve thee as thy hosts a - bove;

al - ways bless - ing, Serve thee as thy hosts a - bove;

12

14

CHORAL SIGNATURE SERIES

Consultant Editor: Simon Halsey

Difficulty Rating ★ ★ ★   straightforward

WORKS INCLUDE:

For further details and a full list of titles in the series,
visit **www.fabermusic.com**

The Faber Choral Signature Series introduces a wealth of new or recently written choral music to choirs in search of fresh repertoire. The series draws in a rich diversity of living composers and includes both lighter and more challenging contemporary works, offering a thrilling array of varied styles.

© Patrick Rowe

HOWARD GOODALL is a composer of choral music, stage musicals, film and TV scores (including *The Vicar of Dibley* and *Mr. Bean*). An award-winning broadcaster and energetic campaigner for music education, in January 2007 he was appointed as England's first ever National Ambassador for Singing. Howard's settings of *Psalm 23* and *Love Divine* are amongst the most performed of all contemporary choral works. Recent works include *Eternal Light: A Requiem*, which was published by Faber Music in 2008 (available on EMI Classics).

ISBN10:   0-571-52044-8
EAN13: 978-0-571-52044-2

FABER *ff* MUSIC

fabermusic.com